Immigrant Gifts

MW01119729

Contents

Listening and Speaking

Listening and Speaking Mat 2

Reading

Fiction

The Aztecs' New Home 4

Nonfiction

Social Studies: Gloria's Gift of Music 12
Science: Alejandro, Dolphin Scientist 16
Math: Immigrants Move to California 18

Writing

Student Writing Model 20–21

Writing Choices 22

Index .24

Our Multicultur

CHINA

CUBA

CUBAN
Black Beans
and Rice

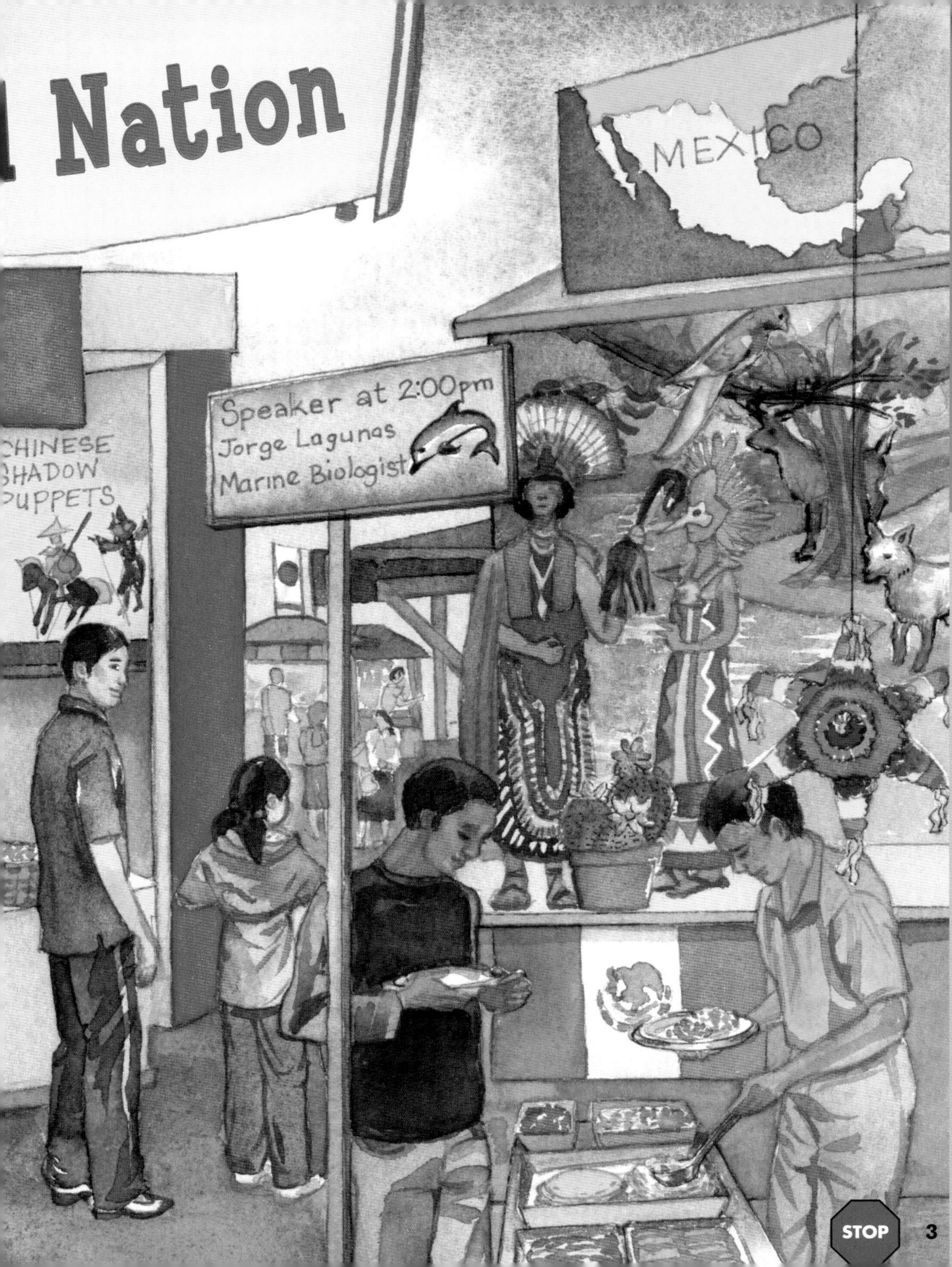
Nation
MEXICO
Speaker at 2:00pm
Jorge Lagunas
Marine Biologist

STOP

The Aztecs' New Home

Long ago the Aztecs lived in a place called *Aztlán* in Mexico. They lived by a lake that had dried up, and most of the plants and animals had died. The people were hungry and thirsty.

One night a wise Aztec man had a dream.

The next morning he told the Aztec people, "Great Hummingbird said in my dream, 'If the Aztecs follow me and move south, then they will have a better place to live.'"

The Aztecs agreed to follow Hummingbird and began walking south. The people were still worried about finding a new place to live, and they became tired as they climbed tall mountains. "Keep going," Hummingbird told them.

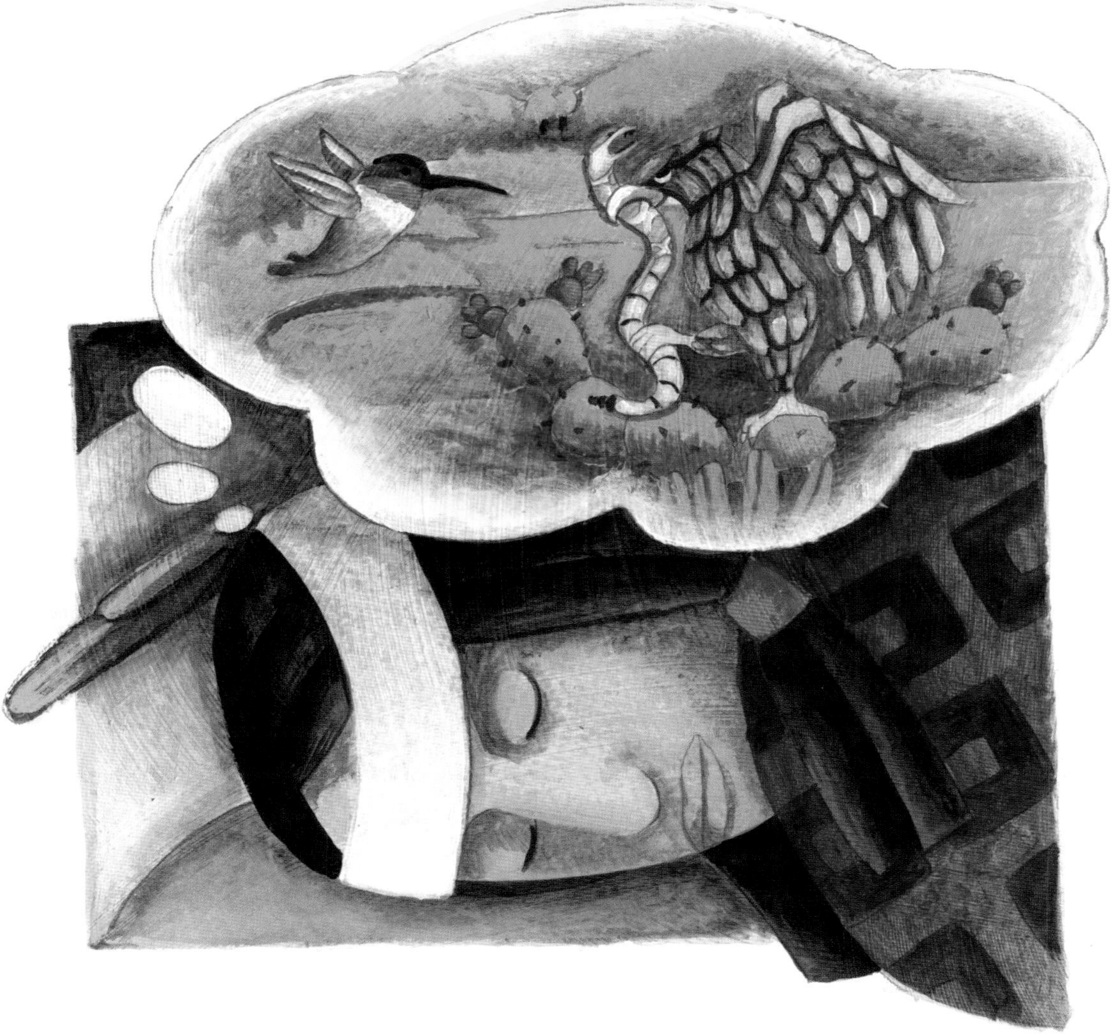

One night the wise Aztec had a second dream. The Hummingbird told him, "You will find a place to live where a flowering cactus stands alone. A golden eagle will be on top of this cactus, holding a snake in its mouth."

The next day the Aztecs arrived on a hill above a great blue lake. They were excited about finding their new home where they would grow crops and have plenty of water.

That night the Aztec people listened to Hummingbird as he told them more about their new home.

"It will be a special place where fish fly, with plants and animals all around."

The next morning, Hummingbird took the Aztecs to the special place by the lake. They saw many fish swimming in the lake and many animals playing near tall trees.

Then the Aztecs saw an island where a cactus stood alone. A golden eagle with a snake in its mouth was standing on top of the cactus.

"This is our new home!" they shouted.

From then on, they always had plenty of water and good land to grow crops. The new home where the Aztecs lived is now called Mexico City.

Gloria's Gift of Music

Gloria María Fajardo was born in Havana, Cuba in 1957, and moved with her family to Miami, Florida in 1959. Gloria's family worked hard, but they were happy to have freedom.

Little Havana in Miami is where Gloria grew up.

Millions of people have seen Gloria sing.

Gloria's grandmother encouraged her to sing to make the difficult times easier, and to follow her dreams. At 17 Gloria began singing and writing Spanish songs in Emilio Estefan's band. She finished college at the University of Miami in 1978. Gloria married Emilio and joined the band, Miami Sound Machine, full-time.

In 1990 the band's tour bus crashed and Gloria broke her back. She could either give up, or she could fight to get better. It took a year for her to get well.

Gloria worked with doctors and exercised to recover from a bus crash.

Gloria Estefan Time Line

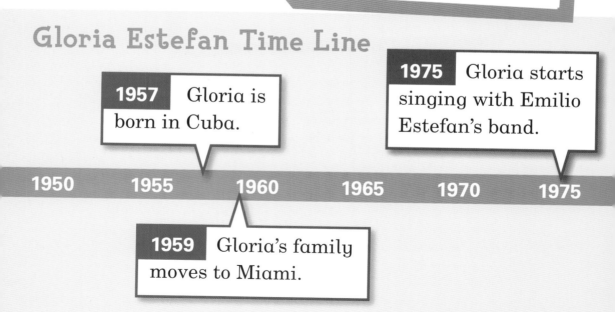

1957 Gloria is born in Cuba.

1975 Gloria starts singing with Emilio Estefan's band.

1950   1955   1960   1965   1970   1975

1959 Gloria's family moves to Miami.

Gloria has won many music awards for her Spanish and English songs. She uses her talent to help people. One of her concerts in Florida raised three million dollars for people who were hurt by Hurricane Andrew.

Gloria has acted in movies, and continues making music for her fans.

Gloria is given an award for helping people.

1978 Gloria finishes college and marries Emilio Estefan.

1990 Gloria breaks her back in a tour bus accident.

1980   1985   1990   1995   2000   2005

1984 Miami Sound Machine's first record album in English comes out.

2005 Gloria writes her first children's books.

Alejandro, Dolphin Scientist

Alejandro Acevedo-Gutiérrez grew up in Mexico City. Every summer his family went to the ocean where he loved watching dolphins and whales. After college he moved to Texas to become a marine biologist. Alejandro's job is to learn how to protect ocean creatures such as dolphins and whales.

Alejandro
Acevedo-Gutiérrez

Alejandro studies
the ways dolphins
work together.

Today Alejandro teaches students about what it is like to be a marine biologist, and encourages people to study and protect ocean life. In 2001 Alejandro received *The National Hispanic Scientist of the Year* award for his work.

Alejandro talks with students.

Immigrants Move to California
by Mito Campo

I moved with my family from Mexico to Sacramento, California. My neighbor is an immigrant from China. We wanted to know if more immigrants came from Mexico or China.

From 1991 to 1998, 3,834 immigrants came to Sacramento from Mexico and 3,455 immigrants came from China.

3,834 Immigrants from Mexico

My teacher told me that the 3 in both numbers is in the thousands place. The 8 in 3,834 and the 4 in 3,455 are in the hundreds place. Because 8 is greater than 4, more people came to Sacramento, California, from Mexico than from China!

3,455 Immigrants from China

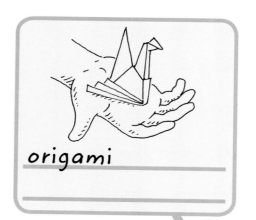

origami

bonsai trees

Topic: traditions from Japan

shamisen music

rice with fish

Traditions from Japan

My family has many Japanese traditions. One tradition is making origami, or folded paper art. We also have bonsai trees. This is another Japanese tradition. Also, my dad plays the shamisen, a traditional Japanese instrument. Finally, we eat rice with fish, a traditional Japanese dish. I like our traditions!

Choose a topic to write about.

Write the topic in the middle box of your web.

Fill in your web and use it to help you write.

Topic: traditions from Russia

Topic: traditions from China

Topic: traditions from Mexico

Topic: traditions from India

STOP 23

Index

Cuba 12, 14

dolphins 16

immigrant 18, 19

marine biologist 16, 17

Mexico City 16

Miami 12, 14

Sacramento 18, 19